PINTS & PULPITS
Devon's Historic Church House Inns

TERRY TOWNSEND

To my wife Carol

For in every sense this is her book, too

First published in Great Britain in 2019

Copyright © Terry Townsend 2019

All rights reserved. No part of this publication
may be reproduced, stored in a retrieval system,
or transmitted in any form or by any means
without the prior permission of the copyright
holder.

British Library Cataloguing-in-Publication Data
A CIP record for this title is available from the
British Library

ISBN 978 0 85710 126 6

PiXZ Books
Halsgrove House, Ryelands Business Park,
Bagley Road, Wellington, Somerset TA21 9PZ
Tel: 01823 653777
Fax: 01823 216796
email: sales@halsgrove.com

An imprint of Halstar Ltd, part of the
Halsgrove group of companies
Information on all Halsgrove titles is
available at: www.halsgrove.com

Printed and bound in India by
Parksons Graphics Pvt Ltd

CONTENTS

TERRY TOWNSEND'S OTHER
HALSGROVE TITLES INCLUDE:

*Once Upon a Pint – A Readers' Guide to the
Literary Pubs & Inns of Dorset & Somerset*

*Dorset Smugglers' Pubs
More Dorset Smugglers' Pubs
East Cornwall Smugglers' Pubs: Kingsand to Mevagissey
East Devon Smugglers' Pubs
East Sussex Smugglers' Pub
Hampshire Smugglers' Pubs,
Isle of Wight Smugglers' Pubs,
Kent Smugglers' Pubs,
Suffolk Smugglers' Pubs
West Cornwall Smugglers' Pubs: St Ives to Falmouth
Wiltshire's Haunted Pubs & Inns*

Bristol & Clifton Slave Trade Trails

*Jane Austen & Bath
Jane Austen's Hampshire
Jane Austen's Kent*

ACKNOWLEDGEMENTS

The thirteenth-century Church House Inn at Harberton.

Thanks to Brenda and Tony Stables for their continued help with proof reading and suggestions

Thanks also to Karen Binaccioni for her invaluable design input

Plus a big thank you to:
All the publicans and their friendly helpful staff;
Reg Howe, Churchwarden at Knowstone for providing access to St Peter's despite the building work that was taking place;
Lyn of the Bradworthy History Society for providing us with a wealth of material concerning Parson William Lang.

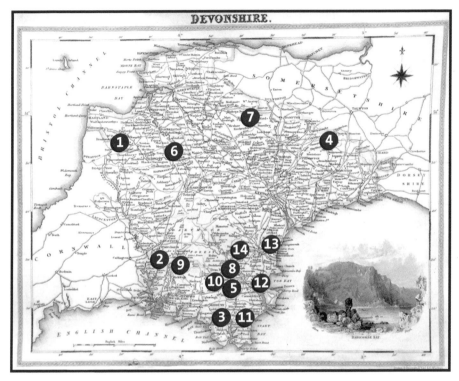

1. Bradworthy, *The Bradworthy Inn*
2. Buckland Monachorum, *The Drake Manor Inn*
3. Churchstow, *Church House Inn*
4. Clayhidon, *The Half Moon Inn*
5. Harberton, *Church House Inn*
6. Iddesleigh, *The Duke of York*
7. Knowstone, *The Masons Arms*
8. Little Hempston, *The Tally Ho*
9. Meavy, *The Royal Oak*
10. Rattery, *The Church House Inn*
11. Slapton, *The Tower Inn*
12. Stoke Gabriel, *The Church House Inn*
13. Stokeinteignhead, *The Church House Inn*
14. Torbryan, *The Old Church House*

Introduction

This is the story of the seemingly improbable marriage between the village pub and parish church. It's a story of pints and pulpits. At the heart of many Devon villages you will find an ancient inn nestling in the lee of a lofty church. Not many sights evoke 'Englishness' more than this timeless tableau and yet the scene is so familiar, few stop to wonder how the unlikely union came about.

People who enjoy visiting old inns often do so because of the sense of history they imbue but this pleasure can be greatly enhanced if the real facts are known. Some inns can feel instantly welcoming offering tantalising glimpses of former times with huge inglenook fireplaces, heavily beamed ceilings and high backed settles standing on flagstone floors. Sometimes there is an internal well or a courtroom where magistrates met to dispense justice.

Church House Inn at Churchstow feels instantly welcoming whilst offering tantalising glimpses of former times with huge inglenook fireplaces, heavily-beamed ceilings and high backed settles standing on flagstone floors.

At the heart of many Devon villages, like here at Harberton, you will find an ancient inn nestling in the lee of a lofty church. Few sights evoke 'Englishness' more than this timeless tableau.

Rev'd Arthur Egremont Dobson (standing), incumbent at St John the Baptist church, Bradworthy, for 47 years from 1911 until 1958. He was the twenty-ninth vicar known to have served here since John Baltyn in 1328 and is pictured in 1922 outside The Bradworthy Inn on the day of the village cricket team's outing. Pub landlord John Grant is standing in the lorry.

Some pubs display a collection of sepia photographs taken during idyllic summers before the young men of the village went off to war. Images of Victorian haymakers, Edwardian cyclists or dusty village roads without a motor car in sight. All these things can combine to provide a general feeling of history that can still leave you wishing: *'If only the walls could speak!'*

In direct contrast to a pub's reticence to reveal its secrets the whole fabric of a village church displays its detailed antiquity. A church can teach you not only about its own history, but also about the history of England. How changes in attitudes to religious practices impacted on social history; how people lived and thought and consequently what topical events were being discussed over a pint of ale in the inn next door.

The whole fabric of a village church displays its detailed antiquity. The altar of the delightful twelfth-century church of St Andrew at Stokeinteignhead was dedicated in 1336, seven years before Geoffrey Chaucer was born.

For centuries churches have been custodians to momentous events in village life like birth, marriage and death but the inn has also had a role. Glasses were raised in the pub to celebrate weddings conducted in the church. Babies' heads were wetted traditionally in the font and metaphorically in the village bar. The majority of memorials in the church and churchyard remember local people who knew both institutions throughout their lives.

Parish churches have been central to the English village scene for nearly 1000 years. In Devon, almost all those existing in 1100 still survive and owe their survival, in no small part, to fund-raising, beer-drinking festivals called 'Church Ales'.

St Barnabas church in Stokenham has, along with most Devon country churches, supplied the central thread in the lives of twenty, thirty, even forty generations.

Church Ales

In the middle ages the word 'ale' not only signified the drink we still know today but also fund-raising social occasions at which it was drunk with the money raised going to the church and the community. Church Ales were held several

times a year to celebrate feast days when ale was specially brewed and a lavish spread was laid on for people from far and wide who came together to eat drink and make merry.

Feasting in 1507.

Early medieval parish churches comprised of two separate sections. The 'chancel' was the smaller part at the east end, which was kept sacred and the responsibility of the clergy. The main body of the church 'the nave' was originally a communal space without seating. It functioned as a secular meeting-place as well as a religious one and its maintenance was the responsibility of the parish, administered through a guild or council.

In Tudor times everyone in the parish, rich or poor, was part of the Church and came together to partake in Church Ales. The community would pool resources for a feast and the proceeds went to maintaining the fabric of the nave and other worthy causes. Originally the festivals were held in the nave where the ale was brewed and food prepared. Merry parishioners would spill out into the churchyard and on to the village green to enjoy sports, morris dancing and mummer plays telling the story of St George and the Dragon. They might also have watched jugglers and bear baiting.

There were various Church Ales including Clerk Ales, Bede Ales, Help Ales and even Cuckoo Ales at spring. Leet Ales were held on the manorial court day and Lamb Ales at shearing time when an especially strong ale called 'lamb's wool' was brewed. Flocks of sheep from a

Lamb Ales were held at shearing time when an especially strong ale called 'lamb's wool' was brewed.

wide area across the Devon hills were gathered together '*to be washed in a flowing stream and then stripped of their burthensom fleeces*'. Even in small hamlets like Torbryan, Lamb Ales were attended by thousands of people.

The word 'bridal' derives from Bride Ales, a wedding feast organised to raise money for newlyweds. Bid Ales were once very common throughout England when general

A wedding procession in 1507. The word 'bridal' derives from Bride Ales, a wedding feast organised to raise money for newlyweds.

invitations were given out and people from nearby parishes were also invited. All those attending were expected to make some contribution to help the object of the benefit, usually a poor person or family or some other charitable cause.

Church Ales were also called Scot Ales, from the Saxon *scot* meaning share. Not everyone however was keen to contribute to charity preferring to buy ale from an ale-wife at a local ale house and drinking it in private. Not surprisingly the Church hated the fact that these people were getting off 'scot free' and decreed ale houses should not brew when the church was holding a function.

The Church held its main fundraising festival at Whitsuntide, which falls in May or June on the seventh Sunday after Easter.

This brewery from 1539 can be seen at Lacock Abbey in Wiltshire. Malt (germinated barley) was boiled in the raised Mash Tun on the left, the liquor flowed down the wooden shoot to the lead-lined air cooler* and thence to the fermenting vessel below where yeast was added.

A Whitsun Ale was a very big affair in most villages. A King and Queen would be appointed for the day and as well as games, plays and dancing there would be archery competitions. The following description of a Whitsun Ale comes from Jefferson's Book about the Clergy:

Opposite: Even in small hamlets like Torbryan, Lamb Ales were attended by thousands of people.

There were no thermometers so an elbow was used to gauge the correct temperature, much like the old style test for a baby's bath water.

'Of the Church-ale, often called the Whitsun-ale, from being generally held at Whitsuntide, it is necessary to speak at greater length, for it is a far more important institution than the bid-ale or clerk-ale. The ordinary official givers of the church-ale were two wardens who, after collecting subscriptions in money or kind from every one of their fairly well-to-do parishioners, provided a revel that not infrequently passed the wake in costliness and diversity of amusements. The board, at which everyone received a welcome who could pay for his entertainment, was loaded with good cheer; and after the feasters had eaten and drunk to contentment, if not to excess, they took part in sport on the turf of the churchyard,

or on the sward of the village green. The athletes of the parish distinguished themselves in wrestling, boxing, quoit throwing; the children cheered the mummers and the Morris dancers; and round a maypole decorated with ribbons, the lads and lasses plied their nimble feet to the music of the fifes, bagpipes, drums and fiddles. When they had wearied themselves by exercise, the revellers returned to the replenished board; and not seldom the feast, designed to begin and end in a day, was protracted into a demoralising debauch of a week's or even a month's duration'.

Up to the early sixteenth century and the establishment of the Protestant religion all the churches in England were Catholic. The churches' final break with Rome came in 1534 with the Act of Supremacy, which declared King Henry VIII as the *'Supreme Head on earth of the Church of England'*. The Reformation gradually led to several attempts to ban Church Ales from taking place in churches and churchyards and, in the later sixteenth century, from holding them on Sundays.

There were efforts to suppress Church Ales altogether under the reign of Henry's son Edward VI but they appeared again under Mary Tudor. The feasts and revels persisted because they were vital to social life in large country parishes and needed to raise money for church repairs and to support the poor. When parishes were no longer permitted to hold festivals in the church or churchyard, church wardens started looking around for a suitable alternative building or building site near the church to establish a community centre where the tradition could be continued. This is the point where the 'church house' enters our Pints & Pulpits story.

The Church House

When John Timpson retired as a presenter on Radio 4's early morning news and current affairs programme 'Today' he began a new career as a writer of books about all things English. His accounts are packed with quirky, fascinating folklore and local historic information. One of my favourites is *Timpson's English Country Inns*. Visiting some of Devon's church house inns he had this to say about Rattery:

'Church House at Rattery is probably the oldest, dating back to the eleventh century. Its spiral stone staircase is said to date from 1030. This is a little confusing since, according to some reference books, it was built to house the craftsmen working on the Norman church, but the Normans did not arrive in Rattery for another forty-odd years'.

Former Radio 4 broadcaster John Timpson was puzzled by the claim Rattery Church House accommodated the craftsmen who built the nearby church of St Mary the Virgin.

The wonderful old Church House Inn at Rattery was established in 1028.

The inviting internal stone staircase in Rattery's Church House Inn is said to date from 1030.

John Timpson's confusion becomes even more perplexing when you consider the majority of church houses date only from the fifteenth century, but several claim to have started life as accommodation for masons building the neighbouring Norman church.

Claims to have been 'accommodation for masons' have validity but are not restricted to the Norman period. They should be viewed against the pattern of building, rebuilding and extending of both churches and inns over centuries, influenced by political and financial factors.

When funds were available parishes usually wished to have as large and beautiful a church as possible so all tenth-century churches were later rebuilt, often extensively and more than once; especially in the 1100s when a number of church towers were added.

In the fourteenth century many churches fell into disrepair largely because of social and economic dislocation caused by the Black Death. Things recovered with new wealth from the wool trade which meant many churches had time and money lavished on them. Several embellishments were made, the most significant being the introduction of aisles to extend the width of the nave. Also at this time a number of church towers which were becoming unsafe were strengthened and extended in height.

In the late fifteenth or early sixteenth century almost every parish in England built a church house. This was the clergy's response to being denied the opportunity of holding ale festivals in the church or churchyard. Church houses were designed with a huge kitchen on the ground floor where ale could be brewed and feasts prepared from food donated by the parishioners while upstairs a large dining hall ran the length of the building.

Finally disappearing in the mid seventeenth century, under the Puritan onslaught against plays and dancing, church houses became redundant. Some were converted to other uses to benefit the parish, like a school for example. Two fine original church houses survive at South Tawton and Widecombe, both continuing their role as community meeting places.

At South Tawton, the beautifully restored Church House still functions as the village community centre and is open to visitors.

This clever illustration by Pat Hughes allows us to imagine the exterior and interior of South Tawton Church House during a medieval Church Ale festival.
Courtesy of South Tawton Church House Management Committee.

Some others evolved into inns after being rented to the former resident Brewster and Housekeeper – usually a female – who continued to brew and sell ale on a commercial basis. Those church houses surviving as inns across Devon today are described by Dr Andrew Swift in *Devon Pubs – A Pictorial Retrospective* as being: *'among the glories of the county'*.

At Stoke Gabriel, worship in the majestic church (seen in the background) is thought to have taken place for 1000 years.

Of the twenty or so still trading as fully licensed public houses those at Churchstow, Harberton, Marldon, Rattery, Stoke Gabriel, Stokeinteignhead, Stokenham and Torbryan retain the title of Church House. Others now trade under more usually recognised pub names like The George at Chardstock, The Half Moon at Clayhidon, The Dolphin at Kingston and The Royal Oak at Meavy. At least three of the church house inns had earlier monastic origins but in each case the building and its proximity to the church made it an obvious choice for secondment by the parish.

For a long time in England the church was inclusive and all the parishioners attended morning and evening services on Sunday. For many living in outlying areas it was not practical to make the journey twice in a day, particularly in inclement weather. The answer was to provide shelter and refreshment, including ale, in a cottage near the church.

A petition in favour of licensing an alehouse near the church at Martock was sent by parishioners to the Somerset bench in 1627, claiming the unlicensed alehouse was conveniently located and necessary for certain members of the congregation: *'sometymes to refreshe them selves in'*, as they lived *'so farr from the parish Church that oftentimes on the Saboth day and other hollydaise they cannot go home & come agane to Church the same day'*.

The reverse of the inn sign at Stoke Gabriel shows artisans of different disciplines working together on a building project.

The pub signs for the Church House Inn at Churchstow and its counterpart at Stoke Gabriel, both suggest the hostelries were associated with the men building the neighbouring church. The Church-stow sign shows a man in medieval dress working on the construction of an ecclesiastical building. He is laying a wall of stone blocks whilst a monk, shouldering a timber beam, is seen walking in the background passing a stone arch. The reverse of the sign at Stoke Gabriel shows artisans of different disciplines working together on a building project.

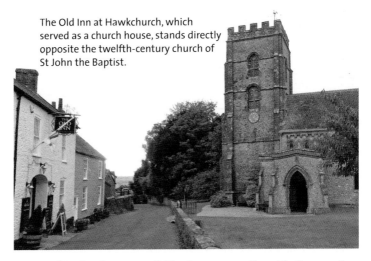

The Old Inn at Hawkchurch, which served as a church house, stands directly opposite the twelfth-century church of St John the Baptist.

Here again the dates are difficult to reconcile with the creation of the original churches. A church owned by Buckfast Abbey had been established at Churchstow by the time of the Doomsday Survey of 1070 but the inn, which was built as a rest house for Benedictine Monks, dates from the thirteenth century. At Stoke Gabriel worship in the majestic church standing above the River Dart is thought to have taken place for 1000 years.

The Masons Lodge

When the term mason is used today relating to building we tend to think of stone masons but a mason in charge of building a parish church was a Master Mason. A highly skilled,

In this medieval painting a mason is seen bottom right using a square to shape a block of stone.

hands-on craftsman who had undergone years of training as an architect. This man also needed the aptitude of a project manager, being able to supervise builders, stone carvers, carpenters, glaziers, roofers etc. In fact, everybody working on a building site was under the supervision of the Master Mason. Testimony to his skill stands today in the numerous cathedrals, castles and churches that still exist.

A Master Mason worked from a Masons' Lodge. Every important construction site would have such a building to serve as workshop and drawing office. All work on the building site was organised from the lodge and it is reasonable to believe it would also have had accommodation facilities.

Master Masons tended to lead nomadic lives going where there was employment. The best ones would be highly-regarded and acquired a reputation. Consequently they would be in demand with neighbouring parishes vying for their services. One way of persuading a star architect to work on your project would have been to provide (or facilitate the building of) a well-appointed place for them to work and stay. Other tradesmen could effectively stay on after completion of a project if there was enough local demand for their skill to allow them to settle. Master Masons however had to move on to their next source of employment.

A reset stone on the façade of The Old Inn at Hawkchurch gives us the date of its original construction in 1547 and includes the most recognisable masonic symbol of square and compasses.

Yesterday is History, Tomorrow is a Mystery

Husband and wife team Andrew Swift and Kirsten Elliott took over a decade to compile their wonderful *Devon Pubs – A Pictorial Retrospective*. This undoubted celebration also includes a lament:

> *'The sight of abandoned boarded up pubs has become as defining an image of the current decade as the sight of abandoned railway lines was for the 1960s. Fifty years hence, will people wax misty eyed at the thought of Britain's lost pubs as they do now for the age of steam?'*

In light of dwindling C of E congregations this sentiment also seems prescient for England's parish churches. Writing in *The Pilgrim's Guide to Devon Churches* Canon Professor Nicholas Orme says:

'Today our churches often seem like millstones round our necks. It takes so much of our time and money to run them. Nevertheless the effort is worthwhile. Parish churches are the Church's best advertisements attracting attention with their spires and towers and bells. They still inspire affection from people, even people who do not come to church. We cannot exist without them: one could say that there is not so much a Church of England as an England of churches'.

The Victorian era saw the last extensive programme of church refurbishment and rebuilding consequently, Hilaire Belloc's 1902 oft quoted warning: *'When you have lost your inns... you will have lost the last of England'* could equally apply today to parish churches as the money runs out to keep them in repair.

From a twenty-first-century perspective well intentioned Victorian restorations have often been viewed unfavourably and described as ruthless, insensitive and heavy-handed. However, not all renovation was purely negative: a side effect of a number of restorations was the rediscovery of long-lost features; for instance Anglo-Saxon carving incorporated into Norman foundations or wall-paintings whitewashed over. Indeed it is true to say without the Victorian's commitment many churches would have fallen into disrepair.

Equally, some restorations of old pubs and inns can seem insensitive when the feeling of antiquity is lost. With profitability the key, the choice is often between having a characterful old pub closing for good or refurbished into a bright, light, attractive family eatery. The Church House Inn at Stokenham is a good example.

Everything in this ancient inn at Stokenham is now light, smart and efficiently run.

Everything in this ancient building is now, smart and efficiently run. In an effort to acknowledge the inn's antiquity, interior designers have removed sections of modern wall plaster to reveal original rubble stone construction. From a traditionalist's standpoint it is easy to criticise but I am pleased it is alive and well and facing a secure future. On the other hand, following a series of bad 'Trip Advisor' reviews the traditional Church House Inn at Holne on Dartmoor is closed as I write and facing an uncertain future.

At Stokenham, in an effort to acknowledge the inn's antiquity, interior designers have removed sections of modern wall plaster to reveal original rubble stone construction.

There are initiatives afoot to save village pubs and parish churches. Village communities are increasingly stepping up to save their local pub as is the case for the former Church House Inn at Little Hempston, now trading as The Tally Ho!

For special parish churches faced with redundancy there is the possibility of appealing to the Churches Conservation

Trust. This charity has secured the future for a number of threatened parish churches including Holy Trinity at Torbryan. Churches under CCT responsibility are no longer used for regular worship but remain consecrated and open to all. At Holy Trinity the charity has mounted an excellent exhibition detailing the church's history and its role in the community.

Another way some pubs are turning the tide is to offer a top quality dining experience like that available at The Masons Arms in Knowstone. The name suggests a possible clue to its origins as accommodation for men who built the adjacent church of St Peter. However, a more likely explanation is the pub was named by the first recorded landlord, retired mason Thomas Snow. At the time of the 1841 census Thomas was sixty-five and running the pub with his wife Anne.

Created from two sixteenth-century cottages with earlier fabric dating to 1400, The Masons Arms is still a village pub where you can pop in for a pint but it is much more than that. The ancient, picturesque, thatched inn is also an award-

winning Michelin Star restaurant. For 500 plus years at least, the view from the front windows has been of the adjacent parish church where, on 28 February 2018 a startling discovery was made.

Some urgent restoration work had been required in the fourteenth-century church building to remove old and badly cracked plasterwork on interior walls close to the altar. A large area of plaster detached and when boards beneath it were removed a staircase was revealed which originally provided access to the Rood Loft.

In medieval churches the chancel screen (or rood

In medieval churches the chancel screen (or rood screen) separated the sacred chancel from the nave. Above the screen was the rood loft, a projecting gallery which gave access to the rood beam (or candle beam) on which the great rood (or crucifix) was mounted.

screen) separated the sacred chancel from the nave. Above the screen was the rood loft, a projecting gallery which gave access to the rood beam (or candle beam) on which the great rood (or crucifix) was mounted. The great rood was flanked by the figures of the Virgin Mary and St John and the whole was accessed via the rood stair.

During the Reformation, King Henry VIII ordered all Roman Catholic icons to be removed from churches and destroyed.

More severe measures were taken on behalf of Henry's young son Edward VI during his short reign (1547-1553) when more damage was done. In 1548, The Privy Council decreed that all the Great Roods should be taken down and dismantled.

In some parishes, the figures of the rood and sections of the chancel screen were hidden by villagers in anticipation of better times. One might imagine the dismay and consternation of Knowstone villagers – including the tenants of what is now The Masons Arms – when a troop of King's men arrived to desecrate their church.

Roman Catholicism was restored during the time of Mary (1553-1558) when surviving rood lofts and screens were back in favour. However, the accession of Elizabeth I in 1558 resulted in the 'Elizabethan Injunctions' requiring any remnants of the previous religion to be torn out and burnt.

Thanks to The Churches Conservation Trust, the redundant Holy Trinity church at Torbryan now houses an exhibition of life in the village over 550 years.

After the decline of Church Ales, church taxes or tithes helped with restoration costs but they were replaced in the 1830s, with the rise of non-conformism. By listing a building, the state puts a moral, if not legal, obligation on the custodians to look after it for everyone. It's seen as part of the nation's heritage and nearly half the listed buildings in England are churches.

This window on Knowstone's history, with the rediscovery of the staircase, was made possible by a grant from the

Fund raising has come full circle in this Cambridge-shire parish with real ale festivals being held once again in the church nave.

Heritage Lottery Fund. Knowstone parish was fortunate to squeeze in as one of the last recipients under the £25m Grants for Places of Worship fund. The dedicated lottery endowment, which churches have relied on for four decades, was scrapped in 2018. Lottery money for maintenance of church buildings will instead come from the overall heritage programme, which supports everything from industrial buildings to Neolithic standing stones. Parish churches can still apply for lottery money within the general scheme but they are now in competition with everybody else, often organisations that have professional fundraisers.

Sitting on the bar of the Church House Inn at Harberton this collection box has the optimistic plea: 'Help us to raise our church roof'.

The Churches Conservation Trust also has a regeneration team delivering major 'new use' projects for historic places of worship which include music concerts and performing arts. In some places around the country the situation of raising funds for the maintenance of churches has come full circle and they are now holding real ale festivals – with dancing – in church naves.

Yesterday is history, tomorrow is a mystery.

BRADWORTHY
The Bradworthy Inn
The Square, Bradworthy EX22 7TD

Tel: 01409 241222

Remote Bradworthy, with its spacious square, was founded shortly after the Saxon conquest of North Devon and is one of the best examples of a Saxon village in the West Country. The Square, providing ample free parking, is the largest of any village. It is remarkable that in addition to Bradworthy

Looking like a quintessential Devon cottage, the building in front of St John the Baptist church is actually the original Church House.

village, there are seven farms within the parish which were Saxon manors recorded in the *Domesday Book*.

With the appearance of a quintessential Devon cottage, the building in front of St John the Baptist church is actually the original church house. By the eighteenth century it had been trading commercially for a couple of hundred years when it was absorbed as an annex to the newly built coaching inn.

A regular customer of the alehouse was William Lang, vicar of Bradworthy from 1622 to 1641. We know a lot about him, thanks to Sabine Baring-Gould's *Devonshire Characters & Strange Events*. As well as parish priest, Lang was a forger and 'threatener', someone we might describe today as a gangster. Numerous charges against him were listed in an article presented in the High Court of Parliament in London 1641 which included: '*He never preacheth the catechiseth* (the principles of Christian religion) *in the Afternoon on Sabbath Days, but*

*goes to the Alehouse, and makes himself so drunk that he can neither
go nor stand'.*

In his capacity as a sheriff's bailiff he
forged several warrants for the arrest
of people he disliked and after obtain-
ing a licence to sell wine he ran a
tavern from the vicarage for four
years. More seriously he conspired to
cause the death of his predecessor
Twiggs and paid Christopher Pugsley
20s 6d to buy rat poison to do away
with four parishioners. The errant
clergyman was eventually imprisoned
in London and is said to have died

there. Some say Reverend Lang was not as black as he was
painted but was discredited because he was a Royalist
supporter.

Georgian stage-
coach travellers
would have taken
refreshment here
while the horses
were changed for
a fresh team.

Facing the Square, The Bradworthy Inn presents the opportunity to step back in time. The corridor leading from the front
door is flanked with elegant reception rooms where Georgian
stagecoach travellers once took refreshment. The corridor
continues passing a staircase with a handsomely carved

During the
sixteenth century
brewing took
place and ale festi-
vals were held in
this area of the
present day pub.

balustrade before arriving at the area where in the sixteenth century brewing took place and ale festivals were held.

Today The Bradworthy Inn is a successful family run business serving good value food where families with children are very welcome, as are dogs. They have two regular west country beers, Sharps' Doom Bar and St Austell Tribute.

Extensively damaged by fire in 1395, the church was rebuilt and rededicated in 1400. Its fine well-proportioned tower, embattled with pinnacles was erected about the year 1500. The Norman font is all that remains of the earlier church. The great oak beam roof arches supporting the unusually broad nave have been described as *'forty arches all askew'*. Village stocks, large enough to punish five malefactors simultaneously, are preserved in the church. The richly carved sixteenth-century pulpit leans like the tower of Pisa.

In the floor are a number of ancient encaustic tiles, common in many churches in this area. They were probably laid about the middle of the sixteenth century and have some interesting

Set in the church floor are a number of ancient encaustic tiles probably laid about the middle of the sixteenth century.

designs such as the Tudor rose, lion rampant, fleur-de-lys and a pelican-in-her-piety. This is a representation of a pelican in the act of wounding her breast in order to nourish her young with her blood; a practice fabulously attributed to the bird which was adopted as a symbol of the Redeemer, and of charity.

A number of village stocks originally erected against churchyard walls were subsequently removed and stored inside the church. These at Bradworthy are large enough to simultaneously punish five vagrants, drunkards and scolds.

Cromwell's troops reportedly stabled their horses in the church whilst on a mission to remove and destroy physical elements and symbols associated with Roman Catholicism. This could also have accounted for the destruction of some early fittings and furnishings. Among the many interesting memorials in the churchyard is a small headstone in memory of John Cann who, according to the inscription, survived all the Peninsular Wars and the Battle of Waterloo before returning to Bradworthy where he died at the age of 101.

Among many interesting memorials in the churchyard is this small headstone in memory of John Cann, who fought at the Battle of Waterloo and returned to England where he lived to be 101.

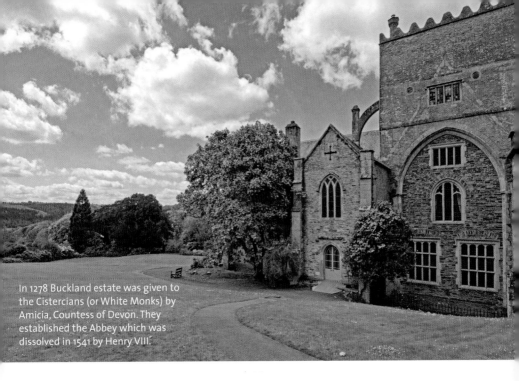

In 1278 Buckland estate was given to the Cistercians (or White Monks) by Amicia, Countess of Devon. They established the Abbey which was dissolved in 1541 by Henry VIII.

BUCKLAND MONACHORUM
The Drake Manor Inn

Buckland Monachorum, Yelverton PL20 7NA

Tel: 01822 853892

In 1278 Buckland estate was given to the Cistercians by Amicia, Countess of Devon. These white-robed monks established the Abbey which was dissolved in 1541 by Henry VIII and sold to Sir Richard Grenville who began to convert the buildings into a residence. In 1581 the house Grenville built on the site was sold to Sir Francis Drake, the great sea captain, privateer and explorer. Following his three-year circumnavigation of the globe in *The Golden Hind*, Drake returned to Devon and made Buckland his home. He lived in the house for fifteen years, as did many of his collateral descendants until 1946. At that time it was sold to a local landowner,

Arthur Rodd who, in 1948 presented the property to the National Trust.

The Drake Manor Inn was rebuilt towards the latter part of the fifteenth century to house the skilled workers engaged on the rebuild of St Andrew's church. When the craftsmen moved on to the next project the accommodation building became a church house where beer was brewed for church ale festivals. The building had its own malting where the barley, in preparation for brewing and distilling, was steeped in water taken from the brook that still bubbles beside the inn garden.

Sir Francis Drake, born in Tavistock in 1541, bought Buckland Abbey forty years later and made it his home for fifteen years.

The heavily-beamed public bar on the left has a chatty, easy-going feel with brocade-cushioned wall seats and prints of the village from 1905 onwards. Beams in the snug Drake's Bar are hung with tiny cups and big brass keys. Horse tack and

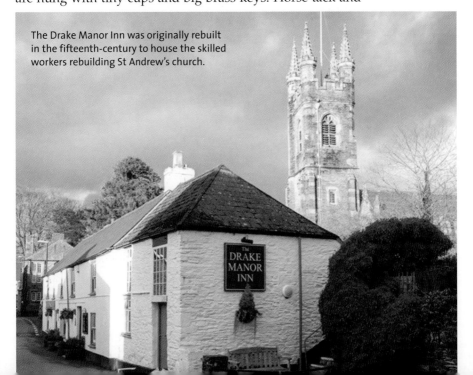

The Drake Manor Inn was originally rebuilt in the fifteenth-century to house the skilled workers rebuilding St Andrew's church.

Beams in the snug Drake's Bar are hung with tiny cups and big brass keys. Horse tack and ships' badges decorate the surround of a large stone fireplace housing a wood-burning stove.
Below: On the right is a small beamed dining room with settles and tables on flagstones with darts and board games.

ships' badges decorate the surround of a large stone fireplace housing a wood burning stove. On the right is a small beamed dining room with settles and tables on flagstones plus darts and board games.

This charming little pub is run by a friendly, long-serving landlady who offers good, very reasonably priced food using home-reared pork and honey from their own bees. Dartmoor Jail Ale, Sharps Doom Bar and Ringwood Boon Doggle are on hand pump, and there are ten wines by the glass, a dozen malt whiskies, 15 gins and three farm ciders.

St Andrew's peaceful churchyard is like a colourful garden.

St Andrew's church dominates the view from the picnic-sets in the prettily planted and sheltered back garden.

Crudely carved from a single block of rough Roborough granite, the old font was probably used from about 900AD but buried for a number of years.

One of the bench ends in the Drake Chapel has a carved globe surmounted by *The Golden Hind* with the hand of God guiding it safely around the world.

A small wooden church was built here in 900 and replaced in 1350 by a more substantial cruciform stone structure. In 1490 the present building was erected with much of the stone salvaged from its predecessor.

The chancel is entered through a remarkably lopsided arch, yet the reason for this anomaly remains unclear. Beyond the choir stalls lies the altar and above this a beautiful mosaic depicting St Andrew who also features in the stained glass windows.

The high roof of the nave is adorned with sixteen finely carved angel figures, playing a variety of musical instruments to accompany the congregation seated below. On the floor of the nave and aisles lies a much admired display of Victorian encaustic tiles, produced by inlaying coloured clays prior to firing.

On both sides of the nave are five grand arches, leading into the aisles, each of which has a chapel at its eastern extreme. The Drake Chapel, is named after the Elizabethan seafarer who circumnavigated the world during 1577 to 1580 in *The Golden Hind*. One of the bench ends in the chapel has a carved globe surmounted by the ship with the hand of God guiding it safely around the world.

In the north-west corner of the church is an ancient Saxon font probably used from about 900 AD. It is crudely carved from a single block of Roborough granite from nearby Roborough Down. When the church was rebuilt in 1490, this primitive font was considered too old fash- ioned to be used in such a modern building and was buried under the church, where it remained hidden for many centuries, before being rediscovered in 1857.

Close to the church entrance, beside a beautifully carved wooden screen, lies the 'new' font. This octagonal structure dates from 1490 and is still in use today. Traces of original colouring may still be seen, together with two carved faces, their tongues out to ward off evil spirits.

The churchyard is a place of great beauty and tranquillity, where blos- som falls over ancient gravestones and bird-song is plentiful.

The list of incumbents includes Walter Weyringe who died of the Black Death a few weeks after he was appointed. Joseph Rowe (1646), Charles Barter (1708) and Richard Hayne (1855) fared much better. They served here for 62, 63 and 65 years respectively.

Church House Inn at Churchstow stands obliquely across the A379 from the church of St Mary the Virgin.

CHURCHSTOW
Church House Inn
Churchstow TQ7 3QW
Tel: 01548 852237

'Stow' is an old English word meaning 'holy place'. It was here, on the apex of a high ridge the Saxons chose to build a church. The medieval ridge road which ran beside the church evolved over centuries into the Plymouth to Kingsbridge turnpike and is now the main A379. The Church House Inn stands obliquely across this modern highway from the church of St Mary the Virgin. This ancient place of worship dates from the twelfth to thirteenth centuries but most of the present building is fifteenth to sixteenth century. The lofty plain tower is a masterpiece with external stair turret all built in faultless ashlar slabs. Housing six bells it is a landmark for miles around.

A board on the pub's façade claims the hostelry is early thirteenth century (circa 1250) and the pub sign itself suggests it was associated with the men who built the church, depicting a man in medieval dress working on the construction of an ecclesiastical building. The mason is laying a wall of stone blocks whilst a monk, shouldering a timber beam, passes in front of a stone arch. Architectural historians dispute the claim, saying the present pub was built as a church house sometime between 1500 and 1520.

The pub sign suggests the building was associated with the men who built the church.

The original building looked much as we see it today except for an external timber stair case leading up the front face to the small arched doorway above the main entrance. This is where parishioner's entered the building on feast days.

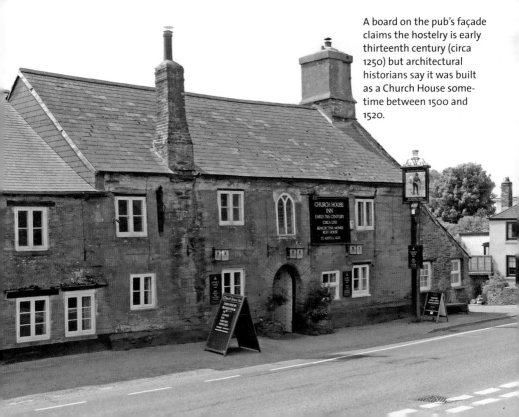

A board on the pub's façade claims the hostelry is early thirteenth century (circa 1250) but architectural historians say it was built as a Church House some-time between 1500 and 1520.

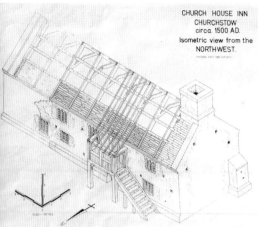

CHURCH HOUSE INN
CHURCHSTOW
circa. 1500 AD.
Isometric view from the
NORTHWEST.

The late seventeenth century saw the decline of the church house during which time the east end of the building collapsed and was crudely tidied up, using a large proportion of the fallen stone, to provide tenements for a poor house. The builders left their mark in scratched graffiti on the outside of the east door jamb with dates ranging from 1695 to 1728.

This architectural line drawing shows a 'garderobe' – medieval lavatory extending from the south-west corner of the building.

In the architectural line drawing the odd looking extension at the south-west corner of the building is a 'garderobe' – medieval lavatory. The present day toilets are in the same vicinity, access is to the left of the inglenook down a small spiral stair.

In the seventeenth century a two-storey building was constructed against the rear of the house. With very narrow windows on the ground floor to keep it cool and a door

To the left of the inglenook there is a narrow doorway leading to a small spiral stair which originally gave access to the garderobe.

leading immediately out to the well at the south east corner with an endless supply of clean water for brewing. It is interesting that this building is used as a beer store today. The well is a metre square and about 10.5 metres deep.

Church House Inn, which has been a hostelry of one kind or another for 500 years, is full of unspoilt original charm

Real ales from St Austell Brewery are served with the confidence of Cask Marque quality.

and character including inglenook fireplaces, log burners and beams a plenty. It has a large accommodating bar, five dining areas and two function rooms. Today the well is a floodlit feature inside a back conservatory which opens out on a terrace with picnic tables and barbecue. Enjoyable home-made food including daily specials and a popular carvery is available Wednesday to Saturday evenings and Sunday lunchtimes.

Today the well, which is a metre square and about 10.5 metres deep, is a floodlit feature inside a back conservatory.

The back terrace has picnic tables and barbecue.

The Half Moon at Clayhidon is squeezed between the lane and churchyard of St Andrew's.

CLAYHIDON
The Half Moon Inn

Clayhidon EX15 3TJ Tel: 01823 680291

www.halfmoondevon.co.uk

Clayhidon's cottages, farmhouses and mills are scattered across folds of the Blackdown Hills rising from the River Culm valley and unfolding northwards towards the boundary of neighbouring Somerset. Clayhidon supported a number of beerhouses which were eventually regulated under the 1830s' Beershop Act allowing the ratepayer to brew beer and ferment cider for sale on their premises. There were also two licensed inns but with the closure of The Hare & Hounds in Rosemary Lane during the 1930s, only The Half Moon remains. This traditional country pub is a real hidden gem, tucked away amidst beautiful countryside surrounded by footpaths just waiting to be explored.

Part of today's inn was the original church house. With its later transition to an independent inn more space was required. The land on which it stands fronts directly onto the lane and is constricted at the rear by the churchyard wall. The only possibility for expansion was laterally but the path between the inn and the neighbouring cottages is an ancient right of way to St Andrew's and mentioned in thirteenth-century records of the church.

A great number of ancient inns have bars and public rooms on either side of their original coaching access. However, the archway at the front of The Half Moon dates only from the 1850s when the footpath was built over to create a large function room above. Once a year on Rogation Sunday (the Sunday before Ascension Day) church officials and members of the congregation of St Andrew's pass through the arch to attend blessings at various points around the village with a hymn, reading and prayer at each.

Today a wide vehicle access runs alongside St Andrew's churchyard and

it even has its own car park but up to 1917 the only right of way to the church was the path through the pub. The function room accessed by an outside staircase, became the centre of parish life used for dances, parties, meetings and fund-raising events in keeping with the original role of the church house.

The function room accessed by an outside staircase. On Rogation Sunday churchgoers pass through the archway beneath to exercise their right of way.

In 1891 the *Wellington Weekly News* carried a lengthy report of AN ENTERTAINMENT held in the function room to raise money for the purchase of new lamps for the church. Miss

The passageway through the pub opens directly into St Andrew's churchyard.

May Clarke, the vicar's daughter, played the pianoforte and sang *'The Village Blacksmith'*. Mr Clatworthy read from Tennyson's *'Marmion'* and later gave a humorous reading from *'Membranous Croup'*. A trio including Miss Braddick sang *'A little farm well tilled'* and later, Mr Culverwell, performed *'I'll place it in the hands of my solicitor'*.

There is an ever-changing selection of real ales.

Miss L. Mildon received an encore following her rendition of the old music hall number *'Where did you get that hat?'* and Mrs Witty sang a comic song, in character *'I'm a young man from the country'*. There were many more party pieces performed by others of the assembly and the evening concluded with all present rising to sing the National Anthem. How I wish I could have been there! Today the room has a stage and skittle alley and maintains its strong association with the church when it hosts wedding receptions and harvest suppers.

There have been several attempts by various owners of the pub to divert the footpath, all of which have proved unsuccessful. The present licensees happily embrace the situation and even supply some free refreshment for the Rogation participants.

The Half Moon remains a welcoming traditional hostelry with a log fire in the friendly bar. There are a couple of separate comfortable dining rooms while outside a collection of tables and chairs, picnic sets and benches are spaced out in the tiered garden across the road with its fabulous views. The pub offers an ever-changing selection of real ales and an excellent mix of traditional and contemporary cuisine.

This welcoming traditional hostelry with a log fire in the friendly bar and a couple of separate comfortable dining rooms draws people from miles around.

Built around 800 years ago, St Andrew's church stands on one of the highest points in the Blackdown Hills. The gargoyles springing from the tower are frightening, like evil spirits trying to escape from the hallowed building. One grim demon is devouring a man held in its relentless clutches.

The fabulous views from the pub garden are simply outstanding.

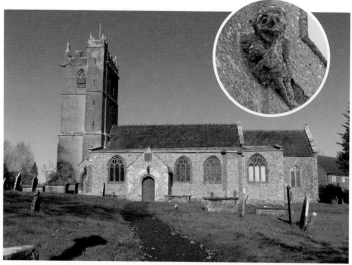

Built nearly 800 years ago St Andrew's church stands on one of the highest points in the Blackdown Hills.

Inset: The frightening gargoyles springing from the tower include this grim demon devouring a man held in its relentless clutches.

There are carved flowers around the bowl of the ancient font and the sixteenth-century pulpit is certainly noteworthy but it is the battered effigy in a dim recess that intrigues the visitor. This is thought to be Ralph de Hidon, the first recorded rector of the parish. People of Clayhidon and passing pilgrims have gazed on this recumbent figure from the time Magna Carta was signed. S.H.Burton in *Devon Villages* has commented that, although its features are gone: *'it stares the gazer out of countenance, bearing so dreadful a weight of years'.*

The beautifully-carved pulpit was installed during the first half of the seventeenth-century.

The thirteenth-century font is constructed of Ham Hill stone.

Church House Inn and the present church of St Andrew's with its 78' bell tower both date to around 1100. The inn is said to have been built as a chantry house and later used to accommodate monks and craftsmen working on the church.

HARBERTON
Church House Inn

Harberton, Totnes TQ9 7SF

Tel: 01803 840231

The village of Harberton lies in the beautiful Harbourne valley. A stream flows by the churchyard and the timeless scene is completed by a fine old spreading yew casting its shadow over ancient graves. All round are houses of great distinction and Domesday farms like East Leigh, West Leigh and Hazard which means *'Hereweald's Bank'*. At Great Englebourne fragments of the early manor house can be seen and the name preserves the memory of the earliest days of Saxon settlement meaning; *'the boundary of the English'*.

The Church House Inn in the centre of the village was built around 1100 initially as a chantry house which later is said to have accommodated monks and craftsmen working on the adjacent church of St Andrew's. The ground floor consisted of a chapel, a great hall which is now the lounge plus a passage-way and workshop, now used as separate dining/family room. In 1327, during the reign of Edward III, the abbot and monks made the chantry house available to be used for the poor. The fact that Church Ales took place here during the seventeenth century is referenced in a document from the Public Record Office, Star Chamber cases, of James I, where gentlemen were tried for serious breaches of local law:

'A Devonshire gentleman, Walter Wooton, defied sessions and assize orders and the opinions of the "best affected sort" in his neighbourhood. "Be of good comfort", he told the villagers of Harberton, …he doubted not but to procure them their church ale, their Whitsun Lord and Lady, their fool and his horns and all again'.

The 'great chamber' of the former chantry house is now used as the bar and main dining room of the pub.

Church House Inn serves well-kept interesting ales including Quercus handcrafted amber ale from Salcombe Brewery and a house beer from Hunters microbrewery at Bulleigh Barton Farm, Ipplepen.

The Church House Inn remained in the possession of the church until June 1950. During renovation work plaster removed from the ceiling revealed fluted beams of mellow oak above part of the great chamber where those early church craftsmen would have gathered to take refreshment.

The two lattice windows in the great chamber lounge are among the earliest examples of thirteenth-century handmade glass.

Plaster also covered a very fine medieval oak 'plank and muntin' screen, composed of vertical 'studs' grooved to accept boards and tenoned into a head rail above and a sill below. Screens of this type were common internal features of late medieval buildings. These non-load bearing partitions were used to divide large halls into smaller cham-

Before restoration, plaster concealed this very fine medieval oak 'plank and muntin' screen, which now separates the long bar with its wood burners from the comfortable family room.

bers or for separating a passage into multiple aisles. This example at Harberton has been identified as one of the oldest complete screens in the country and now separates the main long bar from the smaller family room.

Other historic features in the inn include attractive seventeenth- and eighteenth-century pews and settles plus two lattice windows in the great chamber lounge which are among the earliest examples of thirteenth-century handmade glass. In the entrance hall is a Tudor window frame hidden at the time of the 'window tax', first imposed in England in 1696, and not repealed until 1851. Beside the window is an original map by Robert Morden, dated 1694, which plainly

The church has a two-storey porch with a sundial.

The nave's barrel roof completed about 1370 is aglow with painted beams and 80 golden carved bosses.

Below: The coloured and gilt fifteenth-century rood screen has perfect vaulting but the original wooden panels were replaced in 1871 with metal ones.

shows Harberton but makes no mention of its southern neighbour Harberton Ford.

Today the Church House Inn serves well kept interesting ales including Quercus hand crafted amber ale from Salcombe Brewery and a house beer from Hunters microbrewery at Bulleigh Barton Farm, Ipplepen. There are ten wines available by the glass, plus local cider and good fairly-priced food.

The neighbouring church of St Andrew also dates to around 1100 and replaced earlier Saxon and Norman places of worship. Only the font remains of the original Saxon church and decorative cord-work suggests a date of 1080. The excellent fifteenth-century pulpit has a fine series of miniature figures set in niches. These are probably seventeenth century and Flemish replacements for those damaged during the Reformation. Under the

This very fine fifteenth-century pulpit is one of the best medieval examples in Devon.

present pulpit are traces of steps of an earlier one which may be part of the Norman building.

The nave's barrel roof completed about 1370 is aglow with painted beams and 80 golden carved bosses. The coloured and gilt fifteenth-century rood screen has perfect vaulting but the original

Under the medieval pulpit are traces of steps of an earlier one which may be part of the Norman building.

wooden panels were replaced in 1871 with metal ones. The originals are displayed in two glass cases on the north wall of the nave. St Andrew's has a two-storey porch with a sundial and fine bosses inside on the ceiling, two are of a king and queen.

Only the font remains of the original Saxon church and decorative cordwork suggests a date of 1080.

IDDESLEIGH
The Duke of York
Iddesleigh EX19 8BG

Tel: 01837 810253

Iddesleigh is situated roughly halfway along the famous Tarka Trail which runs between Devon's north and south coast. This hill top village overlooking the lovely Okement valley is perhaps one of the most inaccessible settlements in Devon giving it a real sense of retreat from the modern world. Writing in 1973 S. H. Burton said it gave the appearance of being '*thatchier*' than anywhere else in Devon.

The parish registers for Iddesleigh start in 1541 following King Henry VIII's busiest year when he married his fourth Queen consort, Anne of Cleves. He divorced her six months later before having Thomas Cromwell publicly executed for treason on Tower Hill and proceeding to marry his fifth wife, Catherine Howard, on the same day.

The church house started life in the 1370s as a row of cottages.

War Horse posters decorating the walls are a reminder of Michael Morpurgo's connection with the pub.
Below: One of the former cottages became an alehouse gradually extending to annex the whole terrace.

Exactly a century later, in the prelude to the English Civil War, 92 adult males in '*leddeslegh*' parish signed the Protestation Returns of 1641–1642, swearing: '*to live and die for the true Protestant religion, the liberties and rights of subjects and the privilege of Parliaments*'.

The church house at Iddesleigh started life in the 1370s as a row of cottages accommodating the craftsmen rebuilding the adjacent church of St James. One of the cottages became an alms house (now the pub dining room) another became an alehouse gradually spreading to annex the whole terrace eventually developing into the pub we know today.

At The Duke of York they proudly state they don't have juke boxes, pool tables, fruit machines or karaoke nights: '*We're just a traditional pub serving great food and beer*'.

Today this wonderful old inn built of cob and stone under a long thatched roof is as traditional a village pub as you will see. Despite its remoteness this is one of the most vibrant and popular inns in Devon, with its roaring log fires, barrels behind the bar and convivial long tables. They proudly state they don't have juke boxes, pool tables, fruit machines or karaoke nights: '*We're just a traditional pub serving great food and beer*'.

The Duke of York is author Michael Morpurgo's local and the surrounding countryside is now known as *'Warhorse Valley'*. It was in the pub Michael met the World War One veterans who told him stories of how the local horses were rounded up by the Army and taken off to war, and how only one returned after a miraculous survival. Michael's story of *Private Peaceful* emphasises how rural communities were impacted by the war just as much, if not more, than cities. Generations of young men were wiped out in Devon towns and villages like Iddesleigh.

Other distinguished writers associated with Iddesleigh include poet laureate Ted Hughes who lived nearby and counted the pub as his local. More recently playwright, screenwriter, and film director Jeremy 'Jez' Butterworth rented a cottage in the village. Villagers have speculated how many of the stories Jez heard in The Duke of York ended up

The cottage now serving as the pub dining room was once an almshouse.

From the church door there are uninterrupted views across the lovely Okement valley, now known as '*Warhorse country*'.

in his play *Jerusalem*, described as: *'a contemporary vision of life in England's green and pleasant land'*.

Scottish poet Seán Rafferty moved to Iddesleigh in 1948. In the 1970s his second wife Peggy ran the pub while he took over responsibility for the garden at Nethercott House on behalf of *Farms for City Children*. Ted Hughes was President of this famous local charity set up in 1973 just outside the village by his friends Michael and Clare Morpurgo. Rafferty continued his association with the charity until his death in 1993.

There are excellent wagon roofs in both the nave and north isle. Roof bosses include the traditional designs of the three hares, fox and geese and a face.

St James's church, overlooking the Duke of York, dates from the thirteenth century but is predominantly fifteenth century with some nineteenth-century restoration. There are excellent wagon roofs in both the nave and north isle. Roof bosses include the traditional designs of the three hares, fox and geese and a face.

The modern oak reredos has a finely carved crucifixion under a canopy of birds pecking grapes in its rich vine border, fishes entwined on the dainty crest and two angels guarding the cornice. The semi-octagonal panelled pulpit is early seventeenth century, with an integral carved lectern. There is a Jacobean cover over the octagonal granite font with its carved panels and moulded shaft dating to 1538.

Behind the organ, under a low arch in the north wall is the effigy of a recumbent knight who fell asleep more than 700 years ago.

The reredos canopy is finely carved with birds pecking grapes in its rich vine border and fishes entwined on the dainty crest.

Half of the fifteenth-century chancel screen remains. Behind the organ, under a low arch in the north wall is the effigy of a recumbent knight who fell asleep more than 700 years ago. His head lies on a rectangular pillow, his legs are crossed and his feet rest on a lion. Dressed in chain mail under a surcoat which falls open at the front this knight wore a sword and a shield with no heraldry. He is thought to be Henry Sully an ancestor of Sir John Sully, a crusader who owned the manor at Iddesleigh, where he died in 1387 at the age of 105. The Rev'd John (Jack) Russell, founder of the Jack Russell Breed of terrier, was curate here when his father was rector in the 1840s.

This Jacobean cover crowns the octagonal granite font with its carved panels and moulded shaft dating to 1538.

KNOWSTONE
The Masons Arms

Knowstone, South Molton, EX36 4RY

Tel: 01398 341231

Knowstone stands high on the slopes of the windswept Exmoor foothills. The claim that The Masons Arms dates from the thirteenth century and assumed the role of a church house a century or so later is open to question. For a church house the building is on the small side, comprising of two former cottages. However, beer may have been brewed here and food prepared for alfresco feasts.

Today this characterful village inn is not only renowned for its high quality cuisine, it also functions successfully as a village local.

The building you see today is mostly sixteenth century with earlier fabric concealed. It was extended at the right end in

the seventeenth century and a small single-storey outbuilding was attached to the front right end. It also seems likely, rather than being a reference to the men who built the church, the pub was named in the middle of the nineteenth century by the first recorded landlord Thomas Snow. The 1841 Census for Knowstone shows Thomas and his wife Anne living in The Masons Arms. Thomas's occupation is given as a Mason but by 1850 it had changed to Victualler. By 1861 he is described as Victualler and Agricultural Labourer. By1881 his title has been upgraded from Victualler to Inn Keeper and by 1891 Anne had become a widow and is listed as the Inn Keeper.

The cosy, low-beamed village bar with its huge fire-place retains a cottagey feel.

Today this characterful village inn is not only renowned for its high quality cuisine, it also functions successfully as a village local. In 2005 it was taken over by Mark Dodson, former head chef at Michael Roux's Waterside Inn at Bray. It was actually Mark's wife Sarah who had the vision to see how the formerly rather neglected pub could be transformed into the family-run Michelin-starred restaurant of Mark's dreams.

When Cotleigh Brewery started up in 1979, The Masons Arms was one of the first pubs to sell their Tawny brew which is now one of the most popular beers in the West Country.

A tasteful little lounge separates the cosy, low beamed village bar with its huge fireplace, from the bright rear dining room which has fine views over the rolling hills towards Exmoor and an exquisitely-painted celestial ceiling.

The bright rear dining room with its exquisitely painted ceiling has fine views over the rolling hills towards Exmoor.

When Thomas and Anne Snow were running the pub much of the conversation in the bar would have been about the antics of the local vicar. The old rectory stands next door to the church, opposite the pub where we find another of Sabine Baring Gould's eccentric clerics. Reverend John Froude, who was incumbent here for 48 years from 1804 until his death was described by Devon historian W. G. Hoskins as: *'an unspeakable oaf'*. Froude was an extreme and notorious example of the 'hunting parson', for whom: *'hunting was...the main pursuit of their life, and clerical duties were neglected or perfunctorily performed'*.

Froude was the model for the evil *'Parson Chowne'* in R. D.
Blackmore's 1872 novel *The Maid of Sker* and was, according
to Sabine Baring-Gould:

> *'a parson of demoniac wickedness and craft*
> *who works his will for many years in the north*
> *of Devon, defying God, man, and the law'.*

> *'Froude fascinated his neighbours, overawing*
> *them as a snake is said to fascinate a mouse. If*
> *he told them to do a thing, or to keep silent, he*
> *was obeyed. They dared not do otherwise... He*
> *encouraged about him a lawless company of*
> *vagabonds who, when they were not in prison,*
> *lived roughly at free quarters at the rectory,*
> *and from thence carried on their business of petty larceny;*
> *and who were, moreover, ready to execute vengeance upon*
> *the rector's enemies'.*

A fragment of the former chancel screen is now incorporated into the nineteenth-century pulpit.

The more famous hunting parson, John (Jack) Russell said of
Froude:

> *'My head-quarters (after having been ordained) were at*
> *South Molton; and I hunted as many days in every week as*
> *my duties would permit with John Froude, with whom I was*
> *on very intimate terms. His hounds were something out of*
> *the common; bred from old staghounds – light in colour and*
> *sharp as needles, plenty of tongue, but would drive like*
> *furies. He couldn't bear to see a hound put his nose on the*
> *ground and 'twiddle his tail. "Hang the brute," he would*
> *say to the owner of the hounds, "get me those who can wind*
> *their game when they are thrown off."'*

Situated on a slope overlooking the pub, St Peter's church dates principally from the fifteenth century although the south doorway has an ancient studded plank door thought to be Norman.

Knowstone Rectory, birthplace and home to hunting parson John Froude, stands next to St Peter's church across the road from The Masons Arms.

Situated on a slope overlooking the pub, St Peter's church dates principally from the fifteenth century although the south doorway is thought to be Norman with an old studded plank door which people have been pushing open for more than 500 years. Of note internally is the fifteenth-century wagon-roof and the eighteenth-century communion rails with alternating barley sugar and straight turned profiles.

It is impossible to imagine the villagers' reaction in the early sixteenth century when King Henry VIII's men arrived in the isolated community to desecrate the church. Not only did they remove the Holy Rood, they also boarded up and plastered over the entrance to the rood stair which has only recently been rediscovered.

This illustration is from R. D. Blackmore's 1872 novel *The Maid of Sker*. Parson Chowne, a character based upon Reverend John Froude is shown brandishing a hunting whip at his housekeeper and her luckless boyfriend.

The church of St John the Baptist stands on a grassy knoll above a brook with The Tally Ho just below at the heart of the community.

LITTLEHEMPSTON
The Tally Ho
Littlehempston, Totnes, Devon TQ9 6LY
Tel: 01803 862316

Littlehempston lies in a charming valley where Gatcombe Brook and the little River Hems join forces and flow towards the Dart. All is as it should be in this picturesque village with its cluster of character cottages and ancient stone bridges crossing sparkling streams. The church stands on a grassy knoll above a brook with the pub just below at the heart of the community. Both buildings date from the fourteenth century and both have been saved by the devotion and dedication of the villagers.

The Tally Ho, known by locals as the 'Tally', has been part of village life for around 500 years. Up to and including the Victorian era this traditional village hostelry was known as the Church House Inn and recorded as such in 1830. It was subsequently renamed the Bolton Arms, finally becoming The Tally Ho in 1957.

Standing just outside the churchyard gates is this quintessential church house building with steps to the bar leading down through the porch and outside stairs providing access to the first floor. The historic interior with its thick stone walls, low ceilings and black timber beams is now open plan. There are three open fireplaces, one of which has a wood burning stove providing a cosy place to eat and socialise. The subtle lighting glints off horse brasses, a bed pan, bugle and other shiny paraphernalia which adorn the walls.

All is as it should be in this picturesque village with its cluster of character cottages and ancient stone bridges crossing sparkling streams.

From around 2010 the pub was closed for over three years. To save this historical treasure from becoming private accommo-

The Tally Ho is a quintessential church house building.

dation and to keep it safe for future generations it was purchased by a loyal band of supporters from all over the world. South Devon's first community-owned pub reopened for business on 28 March 2014 and has a special place in the hearts of the locals. Tales abound of those who met their sweethearts, got engaged or had their first drink here, prompting an initiative to collect 'Tales of the Tally'.

The tradition of creating a warm, friendly atmosphere where everyone feels at home is the priority here.

The tradition of creating a warm, friendly atmosphere where everyone feels at home is a priority, as is providing a great selection of cask ales, fine wines and good food made from locally sourced ingredients. The regular beer is Dartmoor Legend with a couple of west country guest ales. The pub garden is tended by volunteers and on warm summer days and evenings provides a lovely place for alfresco drinking and dining. The large free car park behind the pub means parking is never a problem.

The regular beer is Dartmoor Legend with a couple of west country guest ales.

It's not only the pub that was saved by the villagers; the future of the beautiful little St John the Baptist church was secured in 2012 when it was adapted to become the village hall, as well as a place for religious worship. Innovative pews on wheels enables the community space to be quickly set up for a variety of activities.

From the Tally the approach to the church passes by church cottages and crosses the ancient 'pound' between gates where in earlier times horses were tethered during services. The

The church has a Norman barrel roof and font and a wall painting survives in the 'Parvis' room above the porch.

church has a Norman barrel roof and font and a wall painting survives in the 'Parvis' room above the porch. With the exception of the chancel, the church was rebuilt in the time of Bishop Lacy (1420-1455) but three delightful stone figures of two knights and a lady survive from the original. The knights, thought to be members of the Stretch family, are dressed in armour from the 'Camail Period'; a distinctive fashion dating

Three delightful stone figures of two knights and a lady survive from the time of the original church.

The future of the beautiful little St John the Baptist church was secured in 2012 by the locals when it was adapted to become the village hall, as well as a place for religious worship.

from about 1360 to 1405. The camail covered the helmet as opposed to the coif of mail covering the head.

Among many other noteworthy features is the 'Devil's Doorway' set within a split buttress in the north wall and said to be provided for the exit of the evil spirit at baptisms. The church was restored by the Victorians in 1863 when the colourful rood screen was altered and pews and the magnificent Speechley organ were added.

South Devon's first community-owned pub reopened for buiness on 28 March 2014.

The Royal Oak, takes its name from the famous thousand-year-old tree growing by the churchyard lychgate.

MEAVY
The Royal Oak Inn
Meavy, Yelverton, PL20 6PJ

Tel: 01822 852944

The River Meavy runs near this small village situated within Dartmoor National Park, a mile or so east of Yelverton. The Royal Oak, standing at the edge of the village green, takes its name from the famous thousand-year-old tree growing by the

Standing on the edge of the village green this traditional free house is documented as being in existence since 1510.

The pub we see today has the feel of a solid Devon farmhouse with massively thick walls.

Below: They serve good quality locally sourced food in the quiet dining lounge while the very lively public bar provides a Devon welcome.

churchyard lychgate. There was a church owned 'brew house' recorded here as early as 1102 and known as The Church House Inn. The building we see today is documented as being in existence since 1510 and has the feel of a solid Devon farmhouse with massively thick walls.

At some point during the nineteenth century the task of letting the pub was transferred to the Guardians of the Poor of the Tavistock Union. However Meavy Parish retained responsibility for choosing the tenant and since 1974 landlords have leased the pub from the parish.

This popular gem of a pub is a must for fans of real ale, real cider and real conversation.

Although council owned, The Royal Oak is a traditional free house, full of character with flagstone floors, dark oak beams and a large open fireplace. Some of the seats are pews from the adjacent church. This popular gem of a pub is a must for fans of real ale, real cider and real conversation. They serve good quality locally sourced food in the quiet dining lounge while the very lively public bar provides a Devon welcome and a roaring fire. Events include live music and visits from Morris dancing teams plus beer and cider festivals.

Picnic benches overlooking the village green are always popular during summer months.

A stone building for worship was consecrated in the centre of Meavy village in 1122. The present church of St Peter has a Norman core with some thirteenth-century work. The oldest feature of the building is the square north pier to the chancel arch in pink and grey stone. In the fifteenth century the west end, tower, south aisle, south transept and south porch were

The exquisite angel lectern was carved in Oberammergau.

Fifteenth-century features and Victorian restorations both include oak carvings of local wildlife on some bench ends.

added. Prayers have been offered here since monks travelled between the Abbeys of Buckland and Tavistock and the Priory at Plympton, visiting Meavy to celebrate mass.

The third Sir Francis Drake (1647-1718), descendant of the famous explorer's brother, purchased Meavy manor house, west of the church. The family acquired rights over the Lady Chapel and constructed a doorway of granite leading into the passage now called the Drake Aisle. The date 1705 and the Drake Star are carved in the stonework outside. Members of the family are reputedly buried in a vault under the floor beneath the brass plaque on the south wall. The roof of the chapel has some interesting bosses and James Hine, who restored the roof in 1873 wrote: *'One represents a woman's head with a mouse coming out of her ear'.*

Cut in stone between the 'two' altars is a hagioscope or squint. In architectural terms this means any opening, usually oblique, cut through a wall or pier in the chancel. Its purpose was to enable members of the congregation in transepts or chapels – from which the altar would otherwise not be visible – to witness the Eucharist during mass.

In the porch there is a quaint stoup formed from a grotesque head. The roof has gilded bosses and the fifteenth-century Roborough stone font has sculptured panels depicting the crossed keys of St Peter, flowers and a sword. The nave, aisle, south transept and west tower were added in the fifteenth century. Fifteenth-century features and Victorian restorations both include oak carvings of local wildlife on some bench ends.

In the porch there is a quaint stoup formed from a grotesque head.

The Drake Chapel window was given by Lord and Lady Seaton in 1923.

Rattery's Church House Inn, dating from 1028, is one of the oldest pubs in Devon.

RATTERY
The Church House Inn
Rattery, South Brent TQ10 9LD

Tel: 01364 642220

Close to the eastern boundary of Dartmoor the ancient village of Rattery sits snugly in the hilly country a few miles south east of Buckfastleigh. The name is often interpreted as a variant of *'Red Tree'* and is listed in the *Domesday Book* as *'Ratreu'*.

Rattery's Church House Inn is one of the oldest pubs in Devon if not England. In the twelfth century it housed workers building a stone church to replace the previous wooden structure. In consequence, during the 1400s when the Church decreed to move retail and social activities outside their places of worship, Rattery already had a suitable adja-

cent building. It had stood since 1028 and was now reclassi-
fied as a church house.

Only a few fragments of the present building date back to that
time. Most of the structure dates from the sixteenth century
when, together with the church it underwent major over-
hauls. It is the early parts of the building, notably the spiral
steps behind a little stone doorway in a corner of the bar,
which tend to give the pub its authentic historic atmosphere.
There is plenty of character in the homely open-plan interior
with its massive oak beams and standing timbers. In a parti-
tioned cosy nook at one end is a large fireplace. There are
some padded window seats plus traditional pubby chairs and
tables standing on stone flagged floors and patterned carpet.
Prints and horse brasses decorate the plain white walls in the
bar and lounge while in the dining room is a collection of
historic photographs of the local area.

Dartmoor Jail Ale, Dartmoor Legend or St Austell Proper Job
are all on hand pump. Other drinks include 19 malt whiskies

The close proxim-
ity of pub and
church can be
appreciated in the
view from the
churchyard gate.

There is plenty of character in the homely open-plan interior with its massive oak beams and standing timbers.
Below; There are some padded window seats plus traditional pubby chairs and tables standing on stone-flagged floors and patterned carpet.

and a dozen wines by the glass. Traditional dishes plus daily specials cover a wide range from sandwiches to roast guinea fowl with cherry and port sauce.

The pub, not resting on its historic laurels, is still looking forward. To this end they have just added an impressive modern dining extension. Built in a traditional style incorporating beautiful new oak beams it opens directly out into the garden.

The eleventh-century church of St Mary the Virgin stands on a prominent hill and the spire can be seen for miles around this rural parish. The nave, chancel and sanctuary are believed to date from the twelfth century and they still treasure their Norman font – one of only three in Devon with the bowl and stem of red sandstone and grey stone base. The tower, narrow aisles and probably the transepts were all added in about the thirteenth century. The chancel chapels are fifteenth century and the spire was probably added around this time. The external walls of the church were roughcast in 1823.

It is the early parts of the building, notably the spiral steps behind a small stone doorway in a corner of the bar, which tend to give the pub its authentic historic atmosphere.

An impressive modern dining extension opens directly out to the garden with its picnic-sets on the large hedged-in lawn and peaceful views of the partly wooded surrounding hills.

The eleventh-century church of St Mary the Virgin stands on a prominent hill and the spire can be seen for miles around this rural parish.

The Rattery congregation treasure their rare Norman font although it is showing its age.

In 1870 the Rural Dean recommended the square box seats be removed and replaced with open pews to increase congregation capacity. It seems likely the 'unsightly' gallery was taken out at around the same time and the church opened to the west end.

In 1874 a complete system of internal decorative plasterwork known as 'sgraffito' was applied. This consists of a base coat of dark red, two further coats of blue with a top coat of yellow ochre. The superficial layers are etched away following a pattern revealing the deeper layers of darker colour. 'Graffiare' in Italian means to scratch.

This door opens onto almost a thousand years of English history.

It must have looked spectacular when it was first completed presenting a striking departure from the plain walls which preceded it. In 1909 a portion of the sgraffitto was recoloured and redecorated. The very distinctive appearance with its great colour and warmth is particularly appreciated at Christmas and Harvest Festival.

In 1874 a complete system of colourful layered plasterwork, known as 'sgraffito', was applied and then etched or scratched away.

87

This atmospheric old pub tucked away in the heart of Slapton was originally six cottages erected in 1347 to accommodate the workmen who built the ivy-covered Chantry.

SLAPTON
The Tower Inn

Slapton, Kingsbridge TQ7 2PN

Tel: 01548 580216

Quaint narrow lanes meander through the tiny village of Slapton tucked away among rolling Devon hills. The village lies in a beautiful spot around half a mile from the coast and the freshwater lagoon of Slapton Ley. In the centre of the village The Tower Inn had links with both the adjacent Chantry College and the village church of St James the Great. The inn began life as accommodation for masons who built the Chantry complex of buildings. Most chantry colleges or seminaries established in the fourteenth century were commissioned by wealthy landowners who were responding

All that remains today of the Chantry is the 80'
high Belfry Tower and a few masonry fragments
in the late Georgian house called The Priory.

Church pews, scrubbed pine table, bare boards and exposed stone all complement the relaxed atmosphere in this unpretentious pub.
Below: The focus here is on food and the seasonal changing imaginative menu includes fresh fish from the bay.

to the core Catholic belief that the more people who prayed for a deceased person's soul, the less time the departed would have to stay in purgatory.

The old stables have been incorporated to extend the dining area.

The Slapton Seminary, which comprised a perpetual Chantry of five priests, one rector and four clerks was founded in 1372 by Sir Guy de Bryan. 1534 marked the beginning of the end of the College and Chantry, as acknowledgement to the King's supremacy of the Church was now demanded. The College and Chantry were dissolved and surrendered by the rector

and fellows on 17 November 1545. All the buildings were demolished except the gatehouse and belfry tower. The gatehouse was more or less destroyed by villagers in the eighteenth century taking stone to rebuild their cottages. All that remains now is the 80' high Belfry Tower and a few masonry fragments in the late Georgian house called The Priory. When the Chantry was dissolved The Tower Inn would have served as a church house for St James the Great.

Changing beers at The Tower Inn include Butcombe Gold, South Hams Wild Blonde and St Austell Tribute plus their own Tower Best.

This atmospheric old pub tucked away in the heart of Slapton was originally six cottages erected in 1347 to accommodate the workmen building the now ivy-covered Chantry. The pub is now split into four areas, the low ceilinged beamed bar has a very relaxed atmosphere. Throughout there are armchairs, low-backed settles and scrubbed oak tables standing on flagstone floors or bare boards. There are open fires and a genuine core of chatty locals.

Changing beers at The Tower Inn include Butcombe Gold, South Hams Wild Blonde, St Austell Proper Job and Tribute plus their own Tower Best. They also serve local cider and several wines by the glass. The focus here is on food and the seasonal changing imaginative menu includes fresh fish from the bay.

The pub's secluded beer garden, with its view of the Chantry Tower, is a delightful spot to while away the hours on a sunny day.

The pub's secluded beer garden, with its view of the Belfry Tower, is a delightful spot to while away the hours on a sunny day. Sadly the tower can only be admired from afar as it is closed to the public. Centuries of neglect mean the rest of the

The Belfry Tower was an ever present feature in the lives of the parishioners buried in St James' churchyard.

Below: The parvis above the porch had various uses as an ecclesiastics' meeting chamber, a schoolroom or a store. During the eighteenth century they were often used to conceal contraband.

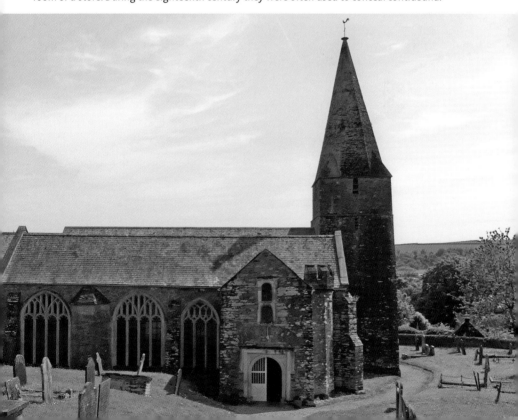

buildings have crumbled away and the tower itself is not safe to visit. There is no roof, and birds can frequently be seen nesting in the upper windows.

The first reference to St James the Great church is in 1292 which means it has served local residents for more than 800 years. Documentary evidence states the church was rebuilt in the late fourteenth century. The high altar was dedicated in 1318 and the chancel and two of its windows date from around this time. The nave and aisles are later than the chancel by about 75 years. The fine rood screen, crowned by a statue of Christ crucified, flanked by the figures of the Blessed Virgin Mary and St John the Evangelist, is an example of how all churches would have looked before the Reformation.

The ring to the right of the latch handle is a sanctuary knocker grasped as a last hope by fugitives from the law.

The church door appears to have two handles but the one on the right is actually a sanctuary knocker or ring. A number of the featured churches have this curiosity. A fugitive from the law, grasping the ring, could claim the right of sanctuary for up to forty days and avoid other punishments if he confessed his crime and agreed to banishment from the country.

After the Reformation it was law for churches to display the reigning monarch's coat of arms.

There is a parvis chamber above the porch. These rooms had various uses, for example as an ecclesiastics' meeting chamber, a schoolroom or as a store. During the eighteenth century they were often used to conceal contraband. Known as an 'Achievement', Royal Coats of Arms to denote the Monarch's position as Head of the Church of England were placed in churches from the time of the Reformation. In this case it displays the arms of George III and is distinctive because the 'artists' are usually anonymous but here at Slapton we know the board was 'painted' by three of the church wardens who have included their names.

The fine rood screen is crowned by a statue of Christ crucified flanked by the figures of the Blessed Virgin Mary and St John the Evangelist as it would have appeared before the Reformation.

Beside the bench-tables on the front terrace the village stocks are a reminder that throughout the middle ages the upstairs room in the pub served as a Court House.

STOKE GABRIEL
The Church House Inn
Church Walk, Stoke Gabriel, TQ9 6SD
Tel: 01803 782384

Stoke Gabriel in South Devon is situated on a creek of the historic River Dart. This unspoilt village still retains its historical links from the impressive 800 year old yew tree in the churchyard to its gentle jumble of cottages leading down to the river where locals have fished for Dart salmon for centuries.

Still owned by the Church, The Old Church House Inn, built in 1152 housed and fed the craftsmen engaged in major rebuilding and renovation work on the adjacent church of St Mary and St Gabriel. This wonderful old pub with its hubbub of daily life retains a quintessential English village atmosphere. The cosy and friendly two bar local is warmed by a wood burning stove in the inglenook. The bars gleam with brass plates and copper warming pans plus horse brasses on the walls and ceiling and a collection of trumpets and bugles. The floors are carpeted throughout and there is a traditional dresser in the dining room in addition to two high-backed settles in the lounge bar. The walls are a pleasing mix of antique timber panelling and painted rough stone with cut in window seats.

The old Church House Inn built in 1152 housed and fed craftsmen engaged in major rebuilding and renovation work to the adjacent church of St Mary and St Gabriel.

The mummified cat on display in the bar was found in 1987

The mummified cat on display in the bar was found in 1987 in the verger's cottage, three doors along from the pub. It dates to the middle ages when it was common practice to

In the truest 'Pints & Pulpits' tradition the pub is still owned by the Church.

The planked ceiling with its expensive fluted beams is representative of an ecclesiastical connection and available church funds.

place a disembowelled cat in the roof space to ward off evil spirits. Estimates of the age of the cat – now christened Cleo – range from 175 to 300 years. In 1963 a cat found in Axminster in similar circumstances has been traced to 1634. The earliest known date for this practice goes back to the thirteenth century.

Beside the picnic tables on the front terrace the village stocks are a reminder that throughout the middle ages the inn's upstairs room served as a Court House. The pub has two regular beers, Draught Bass and Sharp's Doom Bar.

Worship is thought to have taken place over the course of 1000 years in St Gabriel's majestic church looking down on the wooded banks of the River Dart. The thirteenth-century Norman tower was rebuilt in the fifteenth century and restored in the 1850s. The church has a fine carved rood screen and pulpit. Three pew ends have survived since the fourteenth century and there is the most magnificent yew tree in the churchyard.

In addition to a fine carved rood screen the church has this magnificently carved pulpit.

The majestic church of St Mary and St Gabriel looks down on the wooded banks of the River Dart.

Three of the pew ends date to the fourteenth century.

The rood screen has five rows of rich vine carving on its cornice.

On 29 March 2018 Norman Betts, verger at Stoke Gabriel parish church for more than thirty years, received Maundy money from Her Majesty the Queen at a Royal ceremony in Windsor Castle. Norman, whose family has held the role for almost 400 years, was nominated for his outstanding service to the church.

Norman Betts and members of his family have been vergers here for almost 400 years.

The majestic yew tree, as old as the church, leans today on a veritable forest of crutches as its vigorous branches spread across 30 yards.

Over time the pub has extended to incorporate adjacent buildings which laterly housed a wool shop, butchers, carpenter/coffin maker and garage.

STOKEINTEIGNHEAD
The Church House Inn
Stoke Road, Stokeinteignhead TQ12 4QA

Tel: 01626 872475

The village of Stokeinteignhead lies deep in one of Devon's combes, below the southern bank of the River Teign estuary and inland from Babbacombe Bay, just 3 miles from Torquay and Newton Abbot. It is a little secluded place with a lot of thatch and a church on a hill. Most of the village forms a conservation area and there are over fifty listed buildings nearby. The cluster of cottages round the crossroads straggle up the combe towards Upper and Lower Gabwell.

Despite its closeness to the River Teign, the name of the village is not derived from it. In the Domesday Book the district contained thirteen manors which totalled an area of ten 'hides'. The whole area was known as the 'Ten Hide', later corrupted to Teignhead. A hide being the traditional measure

Framed architectural drawings in the bar allow us to understand how the building worked when functioning as a church house.

of land taken to be 120 acres, originally intended to represent an area sufficient to support a household. In Anglo-Saxon England it was a measure of value and tax assessment, including obligations for food render or food rent.

The thirteenth-century thatched pub feels just right with its dark heavy timber beams and inglenook fireplaces. Padded window seats are set in thick stone walls and old timber settles and upholstered benches stand today on plush carpet which covers timeworn floors.

Two regular West Country beers, Otter Ale and Sharp's Doom Bar are on hand pump. There is a separate restaurant area with a quality menu, using locally sourced produce. At the

Renovation work following the 1994 thatch fire led to the discovery of a huge internal fireplace.

rear of the pub, over the stream, is a pleasant beer garden overseen by the church of St Andrew on its high eminence.

The delightful church with its distinguishable wagon shaped roof was built in about AD 1270 and originally consisted of nave and chancel only. The altar was dedicated in 1336, seven years before Geoffrey Chaucer was born. Red sandstone pillars supporting the nave roof are topped with finely carved capitals of white Beer stone where men's faces peep from foliage.

Other interesting features include the fine oak chancel screen dating from the time of Richard II, added around the time the

Antique settles and benches stand on plush carpet covering the timeworn floors.

Below: The inglenook at the far end of the bar area is an impressive feature.

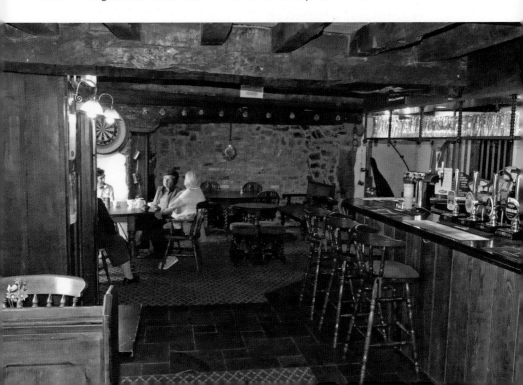

The twelfth-century church of St Andrew rises high on an eminence directly behind the pub.

The lovely chancel screen was added in the thirteenth-century, around the time The Church House Inn was built. It still retains its border of golden leaves and birds in the vine.

Church House Inn was built. It is believed to be the oldest in the county. Unfortunately the screen has lost its ancient paintings but still retains its border of golden leaves and birds in the vine.

The sanctuary is paved with mosaics laid down by Italian craftsmen and a splendid brass portrait from Chaucer's day is set in a step by the altar. The aisles were added during the fifteenth century and a delightful seventeenth-century heart-shaped brass in front of the pulpit has curious engravings of a skull and crossbones, Time's scythe and hour glass with an inscription in early French. It marks the grave of Elizabeth Furlong, whose family owned the Manor of Gabwell.

Red sandstone pillars which support the nave roof date from 1336 and are topped with finely carved capitals of white Beer stone where men's faces peep from foliage.

In 1538 Henry VIII's government ordered a book to be provided for entering baptisms, marriages and burials in every parish. Stokeinteignhead was very prompt in obeying the order and the church registers are complete from this time. The chancel and sanctuary of St Andrew's were rebuilt in 1865 having almost fallen into ruins.

This Grade II listed inn with its friendly welcome has been the centre of the community for over 500 years.

TORBRYAN
Old Church House Inn
Torbryan, Newton Abbot TQ12 5UR
Tel: 01803 812372

Hidden in folds of the South Devon hills, this remote little village is approached along typically narrow Devon lanes. Arriving in the isolated, wooded valley, does not prepare you for a building of such size and grandeur as Holy Trinity church and the delight of discovering its neighbour: the Old Church House Inn, one of oldest and least changed hostelries in Devon.

Built in the late fifteenth century, at the same time as the church, this Grade II listed inn with its friendly welcome has been the centre of the community for over 500 years. Sir John Betjeman passed this way and confirmed what looks like an upstairs window was originally a door to the upper storey, approached by outside steps which have long since disappeared.

The particularly attractive bustling bar on the right of the door is neatly kept. There are benches built into fine oak panelling as well as a cushioned high-backed settle and small leather-backed

seats around its large log fire. On the left there's a series of discreetly lit lounges, one with a splendid deep inglenook fireplace gleaming with horse brasses and incorporating a single side bread oven. The wealth of historical artefacts in this lovely pub give a sense of continuity with generations long gone. Here, hanging from an ancient fluted beam, you will find heavy Elizabethan bowling pins, like those used by Drake anticipating the Spanish Armada.

Built in the late fifteenth century, at the same time as the church, the Old Church House Inn is one of the oldest and least changed hostelries in Devon.

One of the discreetly lit lounges has this splendid deep Tudor inglenook fireplace with a single side bread oven and gleaming horse brasses.

There is also a Tudor recycling variation here. A number of ancient inns have timbers reclaimed from wooden ships but at Torbryan the oak panelling covering one wall of the bar is thought to have come from a sea captain's cabin. There are scored marks in a couple of places where objects (keys and/or a lantern?) have swung rhythmically against the ship's movement.

Elizabethan bowling pins, like those used by Drake anticipating the Spanish Armada, hang from a fluted beam.

It has been suggested this oak panelled wall may have come from a sea captain's cabin.

In the nineteenth century, sheep shearing contests and steeplechases, held in the field at the back, attracted entrants and spectators from miles around. On 23 January 1847 the *Western Times* reported: '*the Torbryan Annual Ball took place at Mr R Pawley's Church House Inn on Monday last. It was attended by many respectable persons from Torbryan and the adjoining neighbourhood. The evening was spent in the greatest harmony.*'

The inn is popular with village residents and guests. They have an excellent restaurant serving local, well-liked tasty seasonal food. Several wines by the glass are available and real ales are from St Austell, Skinners and Hunters' Bulleigh Barton Farm microbrewery.

Holy Trinity is now a redundant church maintained by the Churches Conservation Trust where the charity has established an informative permanent exhibition detailing every aspect of the church's history including its relationship with the adjacent pub.

Score marks in a couple of places on the timber-panelled wall are thought to have been made by metal objects swinging against the ship's movement.

Although an earlier church stood on the site, the present building is almost entirely from the mid-fifteenth century and has been described as the most uniformly attractive church in Devon. It is a perfect example of the Gothic Perpendicular style and was unusually constructed in one twenty-year building campaign between 1450 and 1470. The superb, soaring tower rises in three stages, and has an octagonal stair turret which forms a dramatic architectural feature.

The church owes its chief treasures to Edward Gosewell, the rector who during the Civil War whitewashed the screen and

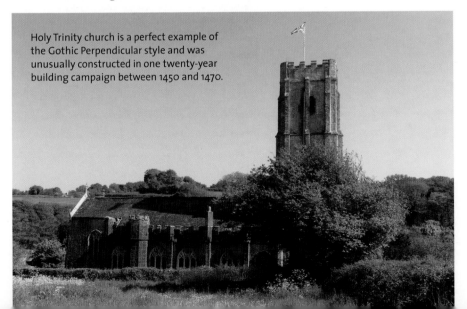

Holy Trinity church is a perfect example of the Gothic Perpendicular style and was unusually constructed in one twenty-year building campaign between 1450 and 1470.

Look carefully at the exquisite and rare fan-vaulted ceiling to see four small angels supporting the central ribs of each fan.

Below: The fifteenth-century oak benches survive encased within early nine-teenth-century box pews. The preservation of the screen and ancient stained glass was due to Rev'd Edward Gosewell, rector here during the Civil War.

buried the stained glass until he was sure a Stuart king was safely returned to the throne. Fittingly, Gosewell is buried with his father, the rector before him, in front of the altar in the church they both served so well.

As you enter look up at the exquisite rare fan-vaulted ceiling with four small angels supporting the central ribs of each fan. The white Beer stone arcades, the plastered walls and ceilings and the uninterrupted light coming through large windows of clear glass make a perfect setting for the screen, pulpit and the exceptional carved woodwork of the altar table.

The fifteenth-century oak benches survive encased within early nineteenth-century box pews all with brass candle holders. The delicacy of the wood carving is echoed by the elegant tracery of the windows, many containing medieval stained glass. Parts of the original rood screen were reused, probably in the early nineteenth century, to form the pulpit, while at the same time the original pulpit was reconstructed as the altar.

Parts of the original rood screen were reused, probably in the early nineteenth century, to form the pulpit, while at the same time the original pulpit was reconstructed as the altar.

BIBLIOGRAPHY

Devon Pubs – A Pictorial Retrospective by Andrew Swift and Kirsten Elliott

The English Pub a History by Peter Haydon

The Pilgrim's Guide to Devon's Churches published by Cloister Books

Companion to the English Parish Church by Stephen Friar

The King's England DEVON by Arthur Mee

Some of the regulars of The Tally Ho at Little Hempston celebrating saving their pub from closure.